10 Truths of Mergers & Acquisitions

10 Truths of Mergers & Acquisitions

◆

A Survival Guide

Dr. C. M. Cower

iUniverse, Inc.

New York Lincoln Shanghai

10 Truths of Mergers & Acquisitions
A Survival Guide

iUniverse books may be ordered through booksellers or by contacting:

iUniverse
2021 Pine Lake Road, Suite 100
Lincoln, NE 68512
www.iuniverse.com
1-800-Authors (1-800-288-4677)

Illustrations by Mark Baum

ISBN-13: 978-0-595-40208-3 (pbk)
ISBN-13: 978-0-595-84584-2 (ebk)
ISBN-10: 0-595-40208-9 (pbk)
ISBN-10: 0-595-84584-3 (ebk)

Printed in the United States of America

Contents

Introduction

If you've picked up this book, you probably fall into one of three categories of people:

1. Your company has just announced that it is merging with another, and though you are hopeful about the future, you want to know what this change will mean to you and your job over the next year.

2. Your company has just announced it has been purchased by another, and you now fear for your job.

3. You are part of the executive management team at a company involved in a merger or acquisition, and you're wondering what secrets are going to be exposed by this book and how you can keep it out of your employees' hands.

For the sake of focus, this book will speak to the people in categories 1 and 2—really, who cares about the people in category 3? These category 3 people, no matter which side they are on in an acquisition or merger, are always the winners.

You're probably wondering about my motivation for writing this book. Well, over the past fifteen years, I have experienced several different corporate cultures—some good, and some bad. Each culture had its strengths and weaknesses, and over time, I learned a lot about various social and political behaviors in the corporate environment. This book is a summation of what I learned.

I recently spent five years going through a convoluted transaction including an acquisition, a merger, and finally a spin-off to private investors. Names of the companies, products, and markets have been changed to protect the guilty. My old company is best represented as **Dumb**. We were in third place in our market. The company we merged with will hereafter be known as **Dumber**—they were in fourth place. Finally, I will refer to the company that bought us as **Big Brother**, a fitting name for a company well-known for its paranoid militaristic culture. When I say militaristic, I'm not just referring to the suit-and-tie dress code. They were very serious about their chain of command: orders flowed down without question or input from subordinates. The security at their headquarters resembled that of a military compound; every time I visited, it felt like I had to go through an inquisition to get past the front gate.

It's almost hard to believe that all of that could happen in the span of five years, but it did. "A long time ago, in a galaxy far, far away," at least in terms of common sense and business ethics, **Big Brother** put forth about one billion dollars to acquire both my old company **Dumb** and our competitor **Dumber**—one of the largest acquisitions in history.

The goal was twofold. First and foremost, it was to create the largest technology provider—the proverbial 600-pound gorilla—in an emerging market of what I will refer to in this book as Complicated Pipedream Technology (CPT). Second, the merger was intended to open **Dumb** and **Dumber**'s client base to **Big Brother**'s sales force and sell CPT to **Big Brother**'s customers at the same time. Let's see … how was it articulated? To "leverage the synergy of technology and services businesses to generate cross line of business pull through revenue." It's catchy. I give it an 8 because you can dance to it. In all fairness, it was a good strategy, and the words, besides giving you really high scores in buzzword bingo, are actually powerful.

It sounds great on paper, right? But **Big Brother**, the technology company that helped introduce the vision of a computer-driven, paperless society into the business world, unfortunately did not understand the 10 Truths of Mergers and Acquisitions. The plan to acquire and merge two five-hundred-million dollar companies was naïve, and **Big Brother** paid dearly; it was forced to spin off the acquisition in a matter of years amid a slew of other investigations, executive management turnovers, and massive losses in overall market value.

Now that you know the roots of the 10 Truths, it's time to give you a little background on the author. Throughout time, history has been written by the winners of conflicts. From the Roman Empire to the British Empire, the Soviet Union to our own great nation, history seems to reflect kindly on the party in power. It's not much different in the business world: the winning company in an acquisition or merger gets to put forth its claim of all-encompassing supremacy when accounting the moments of significance that have led to its success.

Unlike most documentaries, this book will be teaching lessons from the perspective of the losing side—the side I was on. I accumulated quite a few stories to tell from my position on the losing team, and found that once I started writing, I couldn't stop.

The only payback for me is that history reconciles itself whenever there is a transfer of power. After years of transition, Dumber is now going through its own change in management. Though I would never wish anything bad on anyone, I must say it gives me a feeling of redemption. Shall we say, "What goes around comes around"? The new owners who bought us in the spin-off from **Big Brother** started cherry-picking the management team, slowly dismantling the old boys' network. As a result, the management team who had taken us over will now be forced to learn, as I did, the 10 Truths of Mergers and Acquisitions.

So let me tell you a little more about myself. I was an up-and-comer in our old company, **Dumb**. I was, as they say, going places. *I* thought I was cool, anyway. I was a young professional attending all the big meetings, close to executive management. Unfortunately, I wasn't close enough. Being in upper management was great, but there is a big step between upper management and executive management. When the deal went down, I was left stranded with the rest of upper management in the middle of the firing zone—the no-man's-land between the territory occupied by executives and that held by people who do real work where the war of mergers and acquisitions is really waged.

The sad part for me was that I went into this merger and acquisition truly hopeful for the future. You could say I was drinking the corporate Kool-Aid, but I really believed this was the best thing for our company. In fact, I got into several heated arguments with long-time friends, even with my wife, trying to justify why this was going to be great for everybody. But I was wrong. Sometimes the best lessons have to be learned the hard way.

It would be easy to give you a totally negative perspective similar to what my colleagues and I felt for the first year, but all told, this merger and acquisition proved to be the biggest learning experience of my life. For that I am grateful. Fortunately, the experience ultimately took me to a place where even though I realized I was not going to be the big cheese at work, I could step back and see things in perspective. Life wasn't actually all that bad. I still had my job, and I was over-paid to not work hard. You see, in a merger or acquisition, players on the losing team, like me, get quarantined—put in the penalty box. The net result was that my exclusion from most business activities left me with little to do. Let's just say I had a lot of free time.

I also came through the experience with quite a bit to say about the process of mergers and acquisitions and with the desire to spare other unsuspecting employees some of my worst experiences. Details will follow, but first I want to lay down some truths about the nature of mergers and acquisitions (commonly referred to as M&A). You will find that, after a merger or acquisition, the fates of both management teams and their employees boil down to these 10 Truths. My goal with this book is to help you benefit from my mistakes and lessons learned and prepare you to tiptoe through the minefield of acquisitions and mergers. So grab a beer. You're going to need it.

1

The Truth of Mergers: There Are No Mergers, Only Acquisitions

No matter how big or how small the companies in question, and no matter how equal they may be in market value, product recognition, or similar company culture, someone ultimately has to be put in charge. You may have grand delusions of your CEO and their CEO coming together and holding hands in a marriage of business harmony. And in fact they may pretend to do this for you at your first All Hands Meeting as a sign of unity. In reality, most likely, they can't stand each other and find being in the same room a painful experience. I guarantee that when they walk offstage and go back to the executive suite, the digging will begin to uncover dirt, and the political "mud-slinging" will soon follow.

Unfortunately, unlike in a democratic society where your vote counts, this election will be decided in a back room somewhere by the old codgers on the board of directors. These guys, though they may seem to be out of touch with your business, do know that you can only have one President—whether it's a country, or your company. The codgers figured this out a long time ago. Having two leaders is a recipe for failure: you have a stalemate if they disagree, and nothing gets done. Someone has to be put in charge, and, unfortunately, someone has to hit the speech circuit for ex-presidents.

In the case of our merger, the head of **Dumber** was put in charge. This most likely happened because **Big Brother** had financed this merger, and our newly appointed leader from **Dumber** had **Big Brother** lineage; he had been a **Big Brother** employee decades earlier. The **Big Brother** executives knew him well due to their previous acquisition of **Dumber**. Yes you read that correctly: **Big Brother** had bought and spun off **Dumber** years before—talk about not learning your lesson. Unfortunately for **Big Brother**, putting the head of **Dumber** in charge was a critical mistake that doomed the acquisition from the start. It set the stage for a political battle the likes of which I've never seen and have since vowed never to see again.

I always referred to the two company cultures as Republicans and Democrats who had just signed on for a long, wearisome, and rather shady election campaign. The merger and acquisition political battle is not far different from the political battle that happens every day at every level of government in the United States.

Now please don't take this the wrong way—I don't mean to offend readers of either party, and I'm not suggesting that the cultural behavior I describe in this book is representative of either party as a whole. I am simply trying to draw an analogy between our company's culture clash and the clash between any two parties engaged in a political contest. I'll leave my actual political affiliations open for speculation on the part of any interested readers, but for the sake of this book, I will label the **Dumber** employees as Republicans and the **Dumb** employees, myself included, as Democrats.

Republicans and Democrats will never merge, so to speak, into one party that encompasses the best of both views, because that would require sacrifice. Taking the best of both viewpoints would force the party in power to give up a portion of its core beliefs and heritage. There is always a party in power that is calling the shots, and it is much easier for them not to sacrifice. Thus the divide between the two parties is maintained, which results in a never-ending political battle. This political divide is mirrored in the political behavior between two companies in a merger or acquisition.

In our merger, the Republican head of **Dumber** was appointed president of the new company, and Republicans thereby became the party in power. The head of **Dumb,** a Democrat, gladly stepped out of the way—with a scotch in one hand and a check worth tens of millions of dollars in the other. In addition to his multimillion-dollar golden parachute, he received a bonus totaling hundreds of thousands of dollars and for six months served as a "consultant" overseeing the "merger." So the stage was set for the ultimate trickle-down of power from the president to his newly appointed management team, which transformed this merger into an acquisition.

To help define the new power structure, one of the first meeting topics after the deal was finalized involved getting the management hierarchy on paper. This document acts as the blueprint for how the two companies will be integrated—or not. The initial leadership organizational chart was laid out by our new president. At first glance, I have to say it did look like there was some attempt at defining equality in the new management structure. It was rumored, however, that this gesture toward equality was made only after the new parent company, **Big Brother**, stepped in and forced the president to revise his first draft for more balance. Yes, that's right—the original org chart had **Dumber** people in all the positions of power in executive management until **Big Brother** called foul and demanded it *look* more balanced.

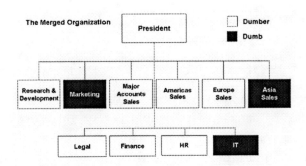

Even after these token changes were enforced, **Dumb**'s management was relegated to three of eleven key positions: marketing, Asia Pacific sales, and information technology (IT). The rest of the executive management team, American and European sales, automotive sales, product development, finance, human resources, and legal, were all held by **Dumber** people. The net result was that **Dumb** Democrats had been effectively isolated while the **Dumber** Republicans had taken over the majority in the house.

It was only a matter of time before the seeds of acquisition, which had been planted under the guise of a merger, grew to fruition—bitter fruit indeed for **Dumb** executive management and their supporting teams.

Don't be surprised. This is how the world works. The clues have been around you all the time. You probably read on a weekly basis that company A is merging with company B. These are merely cover stories for acquisition. They might not be as clever as those cooked up by the CIA for their covert ops, but they serve the same purpose.

For example, HP-Compaq, Sprint-Nextel, National-Alamo, Daimler-Chrysler, and AOL-Time Warner are all examples of mergers that I would bet are in reality acquisitions. Are you really in doubt as to who's in charge over at HP-Compaq? I would assume that Daimler is running the show at Chrysler, and AOL at AOL-Time Warner. If you haven't figured it out, the first clue is simple—whose name is first? I have seen it time and time again, often enough that I've given the phenomenon a title: the First Name Theory.

Here is a clip from the recent announcement of the merger between Sprint and Nextel in USA today.

A highly experienced management team will lead the new company. Gary D. Forsee, currently chairman and chief executive officer of Sprint, will become president and chief executive officer of Sprint Nextel. Timothy M. Donahue, currently president and chief executive officer of Nextel, will become chairman of the new company.[1]

I don't know the parties involved, but I'm fairly certain that this announcement is a polite way of saying that Gary Forsee of Sprint has taken over, and Tim Donahue will be relegated

---

1.   Sprint-Nextel, "Sprint-Nextel Merger Announcement," December 15, 2004. http://sprintnextel.mergerannouncement.com/press/ 12 15 04.html (September 8, 2006).

to a position of no power. Tim will receive a "parting gift" worth millions, then will be put out to pasture after a reasonable interval, free to pursue all the hobbies and interests that running Nextel left him too busy to enjoy.

Over the course of the next year, the Sprint-Nextel transaction will gradually reveal itself as an acquisition in merger's clothing. The Nextel management will find themselves falling prey to the Sprint executive management team as the entire organization is reshaped to give Sprint control.

So take a look at your situation, and read the tea leaves. You can eliminate speculation by asking yourself two key questions:

- **Is your company name first in the new company name?**

- **Is your company president the merged company's president?**

If the answer to either of these questions is no, there are tough times ahead. But even if the wolf is at the door, you don't have to be a sacrificial lamb. Take courage, and read ahead.

Guidelines for Success

Though you may not be on the winning side, there is a chance for survival. Though it will be difficult for you to influence the power structure, there most likely will be organizations which have leaders from your side. Aligning yourself with these organizations will improve your chances for survival. You may believe that you can be clever and get in good with the new guys who are leading your organization, but this rarely works. Trust me. Find an old champion and get under his or her wing.

2

The Truth of Addition: Two Companies Combined Will Not Equal the Sum of their Individual Businesses

Much to the dismay of companies and shareholders, one plus one does not equal two when companies merge. Unfortunately, the process required to overcome culture clashes typically found in M&A has its own mathematical logic. In short, you'll find that 1+1=1 when it comes to mergers and acquisitions.

I mentioned earlier that one of the goals **Big Brother** had in merging **Dumb** and **Dumber** was to create a new giant in the emerging market of CPT. They paid one billion dollars, essentially the equivalent of our two companies' combined revenue, which for those of you keeping score in our home audience, is a clear sign that neither company was very good. Had the two companies really been growing and very successful, the value could have been realistically as large as $5 billion or five times the annual revenue of the two companies. The low valuation of the two companies being equivalent to our annual revenues made us an inexpensive and attractive purchase.

Individually, **Dumb** and **Dumber** were roughly five-hundred-million-dollar companies, ranked third and fourth, respectively, in the CPT market space. We were essentially the Royal Crown and Tab of our market. That's not a good place to be in a mature market, because most markets come down to two major players, and the others get gobbled up. Do Tab and RC even exist anymore?

I digress. The acquisition and merger deal for **Big Brother** was actually the brainchild of our two companies, a desperation play to regain position in a market where we were getting our butts handed to us. The basic strategy was that if we took two companies of equal size and combined them, we'd double in size and overtake the number one and number two companies. Sounds good, right?

Donning some sheep's clothing of our own, **Dumb** and **Dumber** encouraged **Big Brother** to do the elementary math that calculated our combined worth at one billion dollars. The deal seemed logical and low risk, especially since **Big Brother** was valued at over twenty billion dollars. **Big Brother** considered us small potatoes compared to their business, but the deal looked like an easy way for them to expand their business by one billion dollars. If we became more of a blemish than an enhancement to their company, they could always have us removed without dramatically impacting their business. **Big Brother** took us on the way companies hire contractors. Unlike employees, contractors can be let go with no strings attached if things don't work out.

If **Big Brother**'s CEO had had a copy of this book, he would have known that normal addition doesn't work in the process of mergers. Why, you ask? Addition in mergers is different because change is required, or it wouldn't be called a merger. You can't merge on the highway without changing lanes, and ultimately you have to give something up. Usually it is the speed at which you are driving, and often you have to let someone merge in front of you. Did you ever notice during rush hour that most of the traffic backups happen near on-ramps?

This principle also holds true in mergers, and it has direct impact on the business. There is a natural slowdown caused by the disruption of the normal business processes in both companies. At the time of the merger, some big decisions have to be made to eliminate redundancy on the most fundamental of business processes—like administering payroll, benefits, and IT support. All of these decisions create distractions from conducting everyday business.

Our new management team was big on the acronym FUD—Fear, Uncertainty, and Doubt. At the time of the merger, our competitors started spreading rumors about our dim future in order to scare current customers into switching technology and to prevent prospects from investing in us. The merged management team liked to use the term FUD to describe the rumors that our competitors were spreading about us, and they frequently asserted that it was essential to stop FUD.

I don't think it ever occurred to them to use this strategy in-house to relieve the FUD that flies around any company going through a merger. Rumors, driven by people's fear for their jobs, flow from every direction about the fates of every group and person in the company. These rumors can originate anywhere in the company, but typically they come from valid sources and eventually find their way into water-cooler gossip. Unfortunately, this kind of FUD leads to slow traffic at the on-ramp, and the next thing you know, nothing is getting done.

All too quickly, your teams of hardworking people are spending more time on the phone or standing around the coffee machine trying to find out what's going to happen to them. Rightfully so—their livelihoods are at stake. With the wheels of progress slowing, it's hard to maintain the revenue numbers you once enjoyed.

And that's just the beginning. What's worse is that the FUD ultimately reaches your customers and prospects—if not from your competitors, from your own company's vague or inconsistent plans for the future. Either way, it won't be long before the customers who were committed to sending you money and the prospects who were considering buying your product are folding up their wallets until the dust settles on the merger.

A merger leads to a dip in cash flow which slowly becomes a trend. In our case, within two years we had gone from being two five-hundred-million-dollar companies to a combined one-billion-dollar company, but we were steadily inching our way down to existence as a single five-hundred-million-dollar entity. In essence, the merger killed a company. The dream of market leadership had vanished, and we were back in third place where we had started.

What happened to our company in the merger is similar to what would happen to two political parties forced to combine. Instead of preserving the two distinct viewpoints, the party with the most power would eventually smother the weaker party. And that's exactly what happened. **Dumber** eventually neutralized every **Dumb** asset.

The painful part is that we not only killed a company in terms of revenues, but we killed it in terms of workforce. We merged two companies with about three thousand people each into one roughly six-thousand-person company—only to reduce it, through reduction in force (RIF), back to another company of about three thousand.

Mergers and acquisitions are much like the anaconda that swallowed a goat. At first glance, the snake looks, in size, like a snake plus a goat. But over time, digestion sets in and the anaconda shrinks back to its original size. **Dumb** got digested over the course of four years. I sometimes feel like I'm still in the lower intestine somewhere.

Guidelines for Success

You can't directly control or impact the Truth of Addition. The best you can do is plan for it, and utilize it in your favor. Progress is going to grind to a halt. So use your time wisely. Even in a traffic jam after a rock concert or a football game, you can still get out of the car to stretch your legs, have a smoke, or maybe go behind the guard rail to relieve yourself of those last three beers you had.

The same applies for the merger. With the change in management and procedures, you are going to find yourself with enormous amounts of, shall we say, idle time. Here are some good uses for this time:

1. **Produce, Produce, Produce**—Do quantifiable work, and keep track of accomplishments. This provides proof that you're not a waste of space.

2. **Maintain Visibility**—Try to be in every meeting possible, no matter how pointless the meeting may be. This makes you appear important.

3. **Update Your Resume**—You should always have your resume up-to-date anyway, you bozo.

4. **Don't Work Late**—I'm not saying don't do your job, but use downtime to take care of and enjoy your family, or do those projects that you've been meaning to get to.

5. **Exercise**—Healthy body, healthy mind. It just makes you feel better and really helps with your outlook on the situation. Think of it as training for the title fight—the battle for your next real position.

3

The Truth of Division: It's Always Us vs. Them

This is my favorite truth, mainly because it was the easiest to draw analogies from for storytelling. When one political party seizes control of the House of Representatives or Senate, the minority party is left helpless. In a Republican-controlled House or Senate, it is very difficult for Democrats to make an impact on or control the business of government. More often than not, resolutions, bills, amendments, and any other legislative maneuvers proposed by Democrats will get squashed or vetoed. Democrats will find themselves waiting for the next election, hoping the tide will turn in their favor so they can have a majority.

The cultural divide between these parties forces politicians to align with their party and remain faithful. As a result, the party in power considers the minority party members as incompetent and irrelevant, leveraging their power to make them subservient whenever possible. Political alignment is not about right or wrong, but rather staying true to your party, and making political moves to remain in power. In the merger battle of **Dumb** and **Dumber**, the **Dumber** Republicans were clearly on a mission to oppress, and in rare cases, convert, their poor **Dumb** Democrat counterparts in order to strengthen the party.

You will find, as many of us did, that this is the most important and relevant Truth for understanding how things work in the new society. Every decision, every reshuffle, every assignment, every meeting, every reward, every conference call, and every e-mail will reflect the fact that the party in power—Republicans in my case—has taken over, and that, in Republican minds, Democrats should be thankful they did.

I remember the day when I first realized I was Democrat. I had been at the executive summit meeting at our new **Big Brother** headquarters with the top twenty leaders from each company. The purpose for the meeting had been to determine how best to integrate the two companies. It was at this meeting that the new organizational chart I mentioned earlier had been rolled out to the leadership of both companies. We had broken up into working groups, each tasked with coming up with their own strategy proposal for reconciling the products of both companies into a single suite of products. I remember thinking as I walked out of the bathroom during the break that this would be a great opportunity to put my ideas out there. After all, I had been placed in the same group with the newly appointed head of product development for the merged company, who of course came from **Dumber.**

I remember thinking that he seemed like a smart guy, and that it should be a good team. But my fantasies of this merger being a good thing for my company or my career, went up in smoke as soon as the new head of product development opened his mouth:

*"This should be an easy session—your product **Disaster** is a piece of crap, and **Antiquated** doesn't exist. We should have been kicking your ass for years."*

What he was referring to were the **Dumb** products: **Disaster,** our Tech product, and **Antiquated**, our Regulator product. What these products do is irrelevant for the sake of this book. The newly appointed head of product development naturally felt that **Dumber**'s comparable products, **Complex** and **Half-baked**, were superior. It's understandable that people have an allegiance to their products and companies, but I'm not sure that was a constructive way to kick off a group-working session.

Naturally, I felt I had to defend my products. I had been closely involved with **Disaster** for essentially half of my life, and **Antiquated** was a product I had helped launch. So in desperation, and feeling a little bravado, I had responded, "But you weren't … I don't think we ever lost a deal to you guys." This wasn't just trash talk; we rarely had lost a deal to **Dumber.** Of course, we had almost never run into them in competitive situations.

Nevertheless, it wasn't a smart move on my part. Had I said that out loud? Regret over my outburst lingered in my head for months, but it shouldn't have. The battle lines had been drawn long before that day. The head of development, who happened to be Republican, had simply been alerting me to how things would be. It should have been clear that the Republicans had had no intention of jointly defining a product strategy. This meeting had been about flexing muscle and making it clear who held the power. The president was Republican, and power would be distributed down the chain through his Republican associates. If ever a conflict arose, deals would be made and organizations changed to ensure that the Republicans had control of the situation.

Other than that minor confrontation, the meeting had been amicable, though very little was accomplished. In retrospect, I really think the purpose of the meeting had been to size up the Democrats. In essence, the meeting had been an opportunity for the Republicans to determine which **Dumb** employees were hard-line Democrats, which were moderate Democrats, and which Democrats could be controlled. Democrats who didn't seem to know their place would be neutralized either by reduction in force, or like me, by being ostracized. I wonder if they had ever considered the fact that some people were not practicing Democrats, and that the new organization might be best served by forming a new political party, the Independents, and trying to use the best talents from each company. Apparently not.

The merged organization maintained an even balance for about four months. It was as if Congress had been split fifty-fifty between Republicans and Democrats. The atmosphere reminded me of the last hours of an election; both Republicans and Democrats were anxiously awaiting the results in order to see who would win and gain majority voting power.

The political battle had been fully unleashed the day our highest-ranking **Dumb** executive, the ex-COO who had been heading up marketing for the merged company, had been forced out by the rest of executive management. Rumor has it that the executive team and the layer below them had all individually contacted the new CEO (their old buddy) and voiced their concerns that the **Dumb** guy was not a team player. They could not work with him. His removal couldn't have been based on performance, since that would have been difficult to evaluate in the four months he'd held the position in the newly merged company. My guess is that the decision followed an 8-3 vote based on the org chart—assuming that anyone had actually voted.

With our biggest cheese out of the way, replaced by a Republican, the free-for-all had begun. Over the course of four years, the political divide continued to rear its head in the form of disrespect shown to **Dumb** people at every possible opportunity.

Are you in a minority party? Here are some tell-tale signs that might help clue you in.

1. *You are no longer invited to the big meetings*

2. *No one comes to your meetings except people from your old company*

3. *Your travel has been restricted*

4. *Your budget has been eliminated*

5. *Your are not acknowledged when you speak*

6. *Your responsibilities have been reassigned*

7. *Two or more members of the other company think you report to them*

8. *You have been asked to submit a resume*

9. *You have been asked to fill out a job description*

10. ***You do not get a bonus, a raise, or stock options in growth years***

11. ***You are not on any org chart but still get paid***

12. ***Your boss defends leaders in the other company against you***

I could go on and on with this list of clues, but I think you get the picture. The good news is that if this sounds familiar, it's not your fault. There is nothing you can do to avoid this situation. Unfortunately, your job is not a birthright, and the years of hard work that you have put in over the course of your career will all be reset to zero when another political party takes over. That's not to say that you will be demoted, or that your pay will be cut, but the lore of years past, all the great things you have done, will either be lost or tainted because you are in the party with minority control. In our merged company, the Republicans didn't know about the accomplishments of the Democrats, and moreover, they didn't care.

So think of the war at work as a tussle between Republicans and Democrats, Yanks and Rebs, Mac and PC fans, Hatfields and McCoys—whatever you like. But be sure to choose an analogy that makes you smile: you're in for a lot of squabbling, and you'll need something to laugh about.

Guidelines for Success

Be prepared to be treated like an inferior person, or a child. Every interaction with your new counterparts will be based on manipulation and control. Controlling behavior exhibited toward you is all part of establishing the new power structure. Here are a few things you must remember.

1. **Maintain Your Self-Esteem**—This is extremely important because the seemingly never-ending abuse you will take will ultimately make you question your own value. You had value before the merger, and you still do.

2. **Choose Your Battles**—You may win a battle or two, but you're going to lose the war. So avoid squabbles over things that are irrelevant, and defend yourself only if attacks become personal or clearly cross the line. Personal attacks (about your work ethic, appearance, or other matters unrelated to work), especially in public forums, are a form of harassment. They're illegal. But don't rush to play that card. Keep it up your sleeve in case you really need it.

3. **Document Your Conflicts**—Don't be afraid to keep a log of conflicts that are personal in nature. Save e-mail attacks against you. You might need an audit trail for later.

4. **Don't Use E-mail as a Weapon**—Be careful what you put in print. It will be around for a long time. "Flame-Mail" has a tendency to get passed around, and may come back to haunt you. I actually know a guy who got fired for using e-mail as a bullhorn for his feelings.

5a. **Ask Who's On the Call**—When you participate in a conference call, make sure you ask who is on the call so that you can put your comments in an appropriate context. It's very easy to say the wrong things when you don't know exactly who might be listening.

5b. **Make Sure Your Phone Is On Mute**—While we're on the subject of conference calls, follow this common-sense precaution. I have been on several conference calls where I have made derogatory comments to myself about Republicans only to find out that my phone was not on mute. Ouch! Don't inflame the situation.

6. **Don't Complain**—The perception that you have a bad attitude can only be substantiated by the things you say, and once that perception is out there, it's nearly impossible to reverse. Even when you are angry, kill them with kindness. Keep your comments positive—even with your friends. A negative attitude can strain even the best of friendships, and it only makes you look bad.

7. **Be Patient**—Remember, all change takes time. It will take a considerable amount of time for a Democrat to earn the trust of a Republican majority. But don't give up searching for a place where you can add value to the organization. Similar to playing football, keep looking for a hole in the line to run though. The path to daylight might be right around the corner, but you won't see it if you don't have your eyes open.

8. **Keep Your Sense of Humor**—The ability to laugh in the face of hell will get you through the toughest of times.

4

The Truth of Politics: Political Alignment, Rather than Business Strategy, Will Drive All Decisions

If you believe Truth #3, then Truth #4 should come as no surprise. All decisions in the new company will be driven by the party in power. In my case, this meant that decisions were of the Republicans, by the Republicans, for the Republicans. You will probably witness some of the most counter-productive and frankly baffling decisions you're ever likely to see, all of which will be made solely on the basis of what is best for the Republican community, or what best upholds the principles and beliefs of Republicans.

The first and most obvious decision that has to be made in an M&A is what to name the company. Because in our case this was a merger, using all or a portion of our existing company names seemed sensible. According to the First Name Theory, **Dumber** should have preceded **Dumb,** as they were in charge, which would have led to the name **Dumber-Dumb**. It seemed logical and straightforward, but this option was quickly discarded for one key reason: *It had **Dumb** in it.* Though this is a violation of the First Name Theory, some companies like Dumber find it hard to stomach the use of the newly acquired or merged company's name in any form for fear of perpetuating the existence of that company. So the Dumb portion of the name had to be dropped, and the search continued for other possible names.

For a brief time before the new name was chosen, we Democrats got some enjoyment from speculating about it. One of my co-workers had the best idea, in my opinion—take the **bum** from the letters in **Dumb** and the **mer** from **Dumber**, and put them together to form the new company name: **Bummer**. Wouldn't that have been cool?

Even better, since we were a newly merged company that came from the third and fourth place companies in our market, each with essentially no real brand equity in their names, we might have tried a new name. This new name could symbolize the birth of a new company. A new name would afford us the opportunity to cash in our "get out of jail free" card, and drop any bad attributes that may have been associated with these two companies. Additionally, we could truly reposition ourselves and assign ourselves attributes that we wanted for the emerging market.

But, unfortunately, that would have required a loss of Republican heritage. Even though the **Dumb** name had been eliminated, changing our name to something without **Dumber** in there somewhere would be like saying we didn't want to be Republicans anymore. Besides, combining the names might imply the formation of a new political party called the Republicrats, which would never fly in this culture. No, the lineage had to be maintained, and our new company name became something far worse than I had ever imagined: **Dumber CPT Products**. How's that for a mouthful? Can we please get some more words in there?

When naming a company, it's usually a good idea to select a name that is simple, easy to remember, and, although it seems to go without saying, reflects what your company actually does. Let's look at some examples. Cardiodynamics. What do they do? I have no specific idea, but I would guess they are a medical-device business that makes something to do with the human heart. Now for one we all know: Microsoft. It's pretty clear that they have something to do with computers and software. General Motors—GM—does in fact make motor vehicles, from cars, to trucks, to locomotives, to the HumVee. Internet music downloads are provided by iTunes.

Dumber CPT Products, on the other hand, was our company's way of cramming ten pounds of dung into a five-pound bag. Let's dissect the thought process behind this inspired name. It was obvious that **Dumber** had to be utilized in the name since it was the name the Republicans coveted. The original name for their company, before it had been changed to **Dumber,** had actually been **Notsodumb.** Right before we merged, the company had been renamed to **Dumber** to be simpler, and to align with the stock market symbol. Subsequently, the new name had carried no brand equity and had been an acronym that stood for nothing. Since it had stood for nothing relative to the company's products or mission, they had decided to add more to the name to try and make it more explanatory. So the natural choice had been CPT, which was an acronym for the software market we were in, Complicated Pipedream Technology. Of course, not a lot of people really knew what CPT stood for. I'm sure it wasn't on the tip of your tongue either. At any rate, **Dumber CPT** really didn't explain that we sold product, so that had to be added to the name. And so we arrived at **Dumber CPT Products**. But why did we stop there? Something like **Dumber CPT Products For Companies** would have helped describe who was supposed to buy the products, too.

What's really amazing was that there had not been even one person in the "name the company" meeting willing to stand up and say, "Wait a second! This seems a little complicated—don't you think?"

After being spun out of **Big Brother** a couple of years later, the first thing our new owners said was, "Who came up with this name? We're definitely going to have to fix that," and shortly thereafter, our name was again simplified back to **Dumber**. It all came full circle in our merger. We left the station as a merger, and arrived as an acquisition. The best part of the final name restoration had been that even when we had simplified the name, our executive management had wanted to cover up the obvious fact that the name now reflected clearly that this was not a merger, but rather an acquisition. Soon after, the team cooked up a new spin for **Dumber,** labeling it as a new acronym which stood for **D**umb **U**nified **M**erger **B**etween **E**qual **R**ivals. Good one!

What free-thinking individual would actually buy that? What's ironic about that justification is that our executive management had sincerely been trying to bring about some unity between the two companies. But, unfortunately, they too had little respect for their Democrat counterparts, and had succumbed to the general Republican belief that Democrats, like children, are naïve enough to believe anything you tell them.

There's something to be said for the simplicity of true acquisitions: nobody wastes time worrying about silly things like names. If you take over, you get to keep your name. That's the way the world works. He who is in charge makes the rules.

But I would be remiss to waste this entire Truth on our company name. So let's talk about some of the other big decisions that have to happen in mergers.

Integrating two companies is no easy task. Every facet of the business must be considered and evaluated against what is best for the business. Unfortunately, in an acquisition, the evaluation that takes place is more about what is best for the party in power. All decisions, about everything from IT infrastructure to which buildings are kept, are made by the party in power. Whose health benefits package did we get? Which vacation policy? Travel expense policy? Web site? 401-K? You guessed it—the **Dumber** ones. These are important decisions. Just hope and pray that what you end up getting in the transition is better than what you had before. The good news is this is not a long shot. At least you have a fifty-fifty chance.

Another controversial decision was selecting which SAP software deployment would become the basis for maintaining our finances since both companies had used SAP before the merger. For those of you familiar with SAP, you already know about the countless hours that have gone into customizing it for your business needs. So naturally, one of our finance departments would have to go through a major upheaval, and a lot of data would have to be transferred to the chosen SAP deployment. Boy, if that wasn't a debate like no other. That war waged for months. Does it really matter whose SAP system you use? It's data in a business system! Can't we cut and paste from one to the other? Forget logic, because all decisions, no matter how trivial, had to reflect that the Republicans did it better. So you know which SAP system is in place. Welcome to the world of "my dad can beat up your dad."

Even the customer groups had to be dealt with in this merger. With both **Dumb** and **Dumber** having millions of customers from thousands of companies, integrating these customer groups was certain to be a challenge. The funny part was that these two customer groups had been independently managed and run outside of our companies, so their merger really had to be dealt with by them, and guess what? Even the customer groups had had their own version of the Republican and Democrat political battle. What was the debate over, you ask? Well, whose products were better, and whose customer-group meeting was better, of course. The customer group debate was sort of like college football fans. Even though the fans aren't directly involved in the action on the field, they feel a sort of ownership of their team, and will go to battle, in many cases, fighting to the death over their sports team. Similarly, these two customer groups hadn't wanted anything to do with each other initially, and had ultimately been forced by the Republicans to agree to merge. Of course, you know which customer group had been put in charge of the new customer group right? The Republicans Customer Group—of course.

4a. The Corollary of Futility: No Matter How Hard You Try to Change Your Political Party, You're Still a Convert.

The Truth of politics goes hand in hand with what I like to call the Corollary of Futility. I mention this because there are always Democrats in your company who think they will be savvy enough to play the game and convince the Republicans that they have converted from the Democratic party.

Unfortunately, no matter how hard you try to convert, you will never be accepted in the other party. They will always treat you as if you are crashing the party.

Case in point—one of our Democrat product-marketing guys was very shrewd and had realized early on that the product development organization had the power in the new company. So he aligned himself with product development and worked hard to be a Republican Convert. Meanwhile, a Democrat marketing colleague of his had still been thinking that the head of marketing from **Dumb** would run the show. He had also thought he was on the move in marketing, so for him it had been the place to be. So when the first product marketing guy decided to take the product management role in development instead of staying in marketing, his marketing colleague thought he was nuts. Within a year, the guy that had stayed in marketing had found himself ostracized—placed within a marketing group that had no power or influence within the new company. Meanwhile, the product management guy had grown to significant power, managing all of the new Regulator products. Essentially, it looked like he had successfully become a Republican.

Unfortunately, it doesn't matter how many favors you grant as a Democrat on the way up, because it won't help you when the Republican majority decides they want your job. In this case, there was an organizational shuffle two years down the road that left a Republican with nothing to manage. As a result, the ex-Democrat was quickly sent packing so that the Republican could run the show.

I know it seems crazy, but that is how things go. In retrospect, I believe that this person had only been allowed to take this role in the first place because it had demanded an area of knowledge that the Republicans lacked. But once they had gotten up to speed, the time had come to bring in the good ole boys and take things over.

I have another old Democratic colleague whom I heard is still playing the game, and playing it so well that most Republicans don't even know he is a Democrat. But I'm here to tell you that his Republican boss knows that he is a Democrat. I'm sure the boss also knows that he was only allowed to take this role because it was another area of technology that the Republicans do not understand. I expect it won't be long before he too will be ostracized.

Guidelines for Success

Accept the fact that decisions are going to be made, change is going to happen, and most likely, those decisions will not fall in your favor. So plan for change, and be prepared to give up the way you currently do things. Don't get too attached to your environment. Here are a few key things to watch.

1. **Building Consolidation**—You may have to move to a new building—or even a new city—to keep your job.

2. **Benefits**—Your benefits will probably change at the turn of the year. This could work in your favor; you could end up with better benefits. Make sure you compare your current benefit plans and understand the relative differential.

3. **Business Systems and Processes**—You may have a job administering business systems or processes. Keep on the lookout, as change may affect or eliminate your job.

4. **Company Name**—Don't hold on to the past. It's not like they're changing your own name. Just cross your fingers and hope that they don't come up with something stupid.

5

The Truth of Reconciliation: There Are Too Many Products, Something Has to Go

It doesn't matter how good the products of either company are in a merger or acquisition. Something is going to get eliminated. Most businesses don't do a good job of managing their own product portfolios. So when two companies come together, managing two overlapping product portfolios rarely works. Don't kid yourself—something has to go, and most likely it will come from the political minority product line.

A similar phenomenon often happens when a couple moves in together. They both typically have furnished apartments, or houses, complete with bedroom sets, couches, and TVs. When couples move in together it usually means some things have to get displaced. The extra bed must be relegated to the spare bedroom or put out with the trash. It is no different with companies and their products.

So when it came time to merge our two companies, there were clearly a few decisions to be made: we had had plenty of product overlap. The ironic thing about the **Dumber-Dumb** merger was that we sold this merger to our buyer, **Big Brother**, on the principle that the two companies had complementary products. Some of these products had been leaders in their respective categories, and others had been laggards. The strategy for the merger had been to combine the products in order to enable the new company to claim leadership in the CPT market. In theory, our girlfriend had a bedroom set and chair, and we had a sofa and TV set, so moving in together would result in a fully furnished apartment.

The reality of this merger, however, was not so cut and dried. Politics had gotten in the way of rationale, which led to progress similar to glacial movement. To better understand the failure in execution, it's important to understand the landscape of the overlap.

If you stack up the products, they really had had different strengths which in theory could have been used to our advantage. If you break down the combined set of products, we basically had a handful of product categories—Regulator, Tech, Geek, Nerdy, Flashy, and Share products. **Dumber** had been strong in Geek, Flashy, and Share products, while **Dumb** had been strong in Nerdy and Regulator. We had both been about equal in Tech with roughly the same market size and number of customers. However, we both had marquee customers in the Tech market, mainly in the automotive industry.

We had a huge opportunity to leverage our strengths and put together a product strategy that maintained both customer bases while effectively doubling the size of our market share. For example, since we had been leaders in several categories, we could have started by being honest about the strengths of each product and understanding where those products had been sold successfully. The combined company could have claimed leadership in the Regulator, Flashy, Share, Geek, and Nerdy markets. The weak products from both companies in these categories could have been killed with little impact on the bottom line, because they had had very few customers.

This would have left only a couple of products to sort out. The merged company had three Tech products. In the high-end market, we had **Complex** and **Disaster**, which were established, complicated, and expensive Tech products. Killing either one would have been painful, as they had thousands of customers between them. One other point of interest was that **Disaster** had been the Tech leader in Japan.

Our third Tech product was **Blacksheep** which had been acquired from a competitor a few years prior. **Blacksheep** was a much more modern, mid-range Tech product. It was relatively inexpensive, and had roughly 80 percent of the functionality of **Complex** and **Disaster**. However, **Blacksheep** had been all that most customers would need or want. The downside was that it had also been third in the mid-market Tech space, with far fewer customers. On a positive note, customers had started moving away from high-end Tech products like **Complex** and **Disaster** and had been replacing them with mid-market Tech products like **Blacksheep**. Needless to say, reconciling these three Tech systems would be a bit complicated.

Marketing principles would tell you that, first and foremost, major established products like **Complex** and **Disaster** would have to be maintained for quite some time to support existing customers. Extreme care would have to be taken to make sure that all customers could be moved forward over time to our future products as they evolved with technology.

Second, marketing principles would demand that we keep in mind the forces at work, such as the fact that companies had been replacing their high-end Tech products with mid-range Tech products. For example, we had had customers who had been getting rid of **Complex** and replacing it with **Blacksheep**. Additionally, mid-range competitors like **Easy** had been replacing high-end Tech products around the globe. Mid-range products were the next generation in technology—easier to use and less expensive.

This technology revolution was very similar to the changes seen in the video electronics market not so long ago. Our high-end Tech products **Complex** and **Disaster** were like VCRs, and mid-range Tech products like **Blacksheep** and our competitor's product **Easy** were like DVD players. Over the past seven years, consumers have been replacing their VCRs with DVD players at a rate faster than the adoption of any prior technology. Why? Because there is new value with DVDs: they can last for a hundred years without deterioration, the picture quality is better, and you can jump right to specific chapters without rewinding and fast-forwarding. People were not buying new VCRs when their old ones broke. They were simply upgrading to a DVD player. And typically, they'd wait until the VCR broke or until the price point of the DVD player came down from the original five hundred dollars to a better price point—something closer to one hundred dollars.

Similarly, companies weren't replacing **Disaster** with **Complex**, another high-end Tech product. That would have been like swapping your VCR for another VCR. In fact, many companies hadn't been replacing their Tech products at all until they had felt it was essential. My guess is that it will take another five years before customers will be willing to incur the expense of purchasing new Tech product, not to mention retraining their users on these new products. But when they do decide to upgrade their technology, they will move away from the outdated Tech product—a VCR—to a more modern, mid-range Tech product—a DVD player.

These basic facts would seem to suggest an equally basic strategy: don't kill **Complex** or **Disaster,** because customers are not going to switch products for five to ten years anyway. Instead, create a product vision that says the more modern **Blacksheep** is the future product, and that both **Complex** and **Disaster** customers will evolve to **Blacksheep**. In the meantime, we position and market **Complex** and **Disaster** in the markets where they have been successful—as Tech products for the Automotive and Japan markets. Ensure that both solutions continue to be enhanced to keep customers and their revenue. At some point those customers will want to make that move on their own, and hopefully it will be to our mid-range Tech product.

Executing a product reconciliation of this magnitude would have been manageable if either of the two companies had been strong in marketing. Unfortunately, our two companies were weak in marketing. This weakness, combined with the political divide inflicted by the **Dumber** employees, made it very difficult to reconcile the product overlaps. Remember the

Truths of Division and Politics? Those are what came into play here—forget marketing.

Rather than attempting to put together a complementary market strategy, it was much easier for the **Dumber** people to simply eliminate the **Dumb** products, much like they had been eliminating everything to do with **Dumb,** including its people. This slash-and-burn approach to resolving product overlap was the easy way out and delivered immediate results. It is important to note, that the elimination of products happens over time because although you may stop selling a product, customers will continue to use it, and may not consider purchasing a replacement product for some time. This phenomenon became a harsh reality for Dumber as you will learn.

Naturally, when it came to eliminating products, **Disaster** had to be killed at all costs because it had come from **Dumb**—period. **Blacksheep** could not go forward because it had also been the product of an acquisition—a stepchild, so to speak. Since **Dumber** hadn't created it, it couldn't be a better product than **Complex.**

Yes, **Complex** had to be the future product, and all customers would have to move to **Complex.** To make it seem like new technology, we renamed it **NewComplex.** A new name would surely make the **Disaster** customers want to start over with a new product, right? What's funny is that four years later, I can still count the number of **Disaster** customers who have moved to **NewComplex** on two hands. Even God couldn't have made it happen. In fact, more **Disaster** customers have moved to the more modern **Blacksheep**, the mid-range Tech product. That's where the market is going. It's difficult to go against that trend. Unfortunately for us, even more of our old customers had moved to **Easy**, the more modern product of our competitor.

Wait, it gets better—I mean worse. **Disaster** and **Complex**, brands which had been well established in the market space, had effectively been killed and replaced with **NewComplex**—which had had no brand equity. After four years, we had two two-hundred-million dollar Tech products which were declining in revenue at a rate of about 10 percent per year. Now that's good business.

Just when you thought it couldn't get worse, **Dumber** got even, well, *dumber.* The merged company also had overlapping Regulator products. The undisputed leader in the market was **Dumb**'s **Antiquated; Dumber**'s **Halfbaked** was fourth in the market.

Antiquated had over ten times as many customers as **Halfbaked**, as well as the best brand equity of all of our two companies' products. It was well established as a Regulator product.

Halfbaked, on the other hand, had very few customers, and 60 percent of its revenue came from one customer. Logic would tell a normal marketing person that **Halfbaked** probably needed to go, which would have had little impact on the market or our revenue. If we kept it, we could have positioned it as a mid-range product, rather than just a Regulator product. This positioning would have made the two Regulator products appear complementary.

But you guessed it! **Antiquated** had to be killed because it had come from **Dumb,** and all customers would have to move to **Halfbaked.** Four years later, very few **Antiquated** customers have moved to **Halfbaked**, but the revenue stream from **Antiquated** has changed from 14 percent growth to flat.

We've obviously made some boneheaded decisions in reconciling our product portfolio, and all of these have been driven by politics. I remember being in several meetings within the first year where we had gathered product development teams from both companies to evaluate our technologies. The goal had been to compare strengths and weaknesses and utilize that information to build a plan.

Unfortunately, it quickly turned into a contest driven by people's fear for their jobs. People had started believing that if the technology they worked on was deemed lower quality, they would be out of jobs. The discussions had transformed into competing displays of muscle. Both product development teams claimed that their products could do anything and everything. When the evaluation was complete, it was a tie on all angles—amazing.

What a waste of time. If you multiply the average burden rate of the employees involved (approximately one hundred dollars per hour) by the number of people (about fifty), by the hours spent (roughly two man-months), I'd have to say it had cost us roughly 1.6 million dollars to go through this evaluation. This actually was the inspiration for the WasteOmeter, which calculates the cost of meetings. I hope to someday create such a product to help companies stop wasting time.

In retrospect, the product evaluation effort had really been calculated as a show of good will. We were going through the motions and taking the opportunity to size everybody up. They had wanted to identify who could be converted, who could be eliminated, and who would be ostracized. Chilling.

Of course, the more likely, and in its own way, more chilling possibility is that it wasn't a show of good will. These guys were not that smart. There was no way they could possibly manipulate people that well. I think the reality was that they had actually believed (as we'll talk about later in the Truth of Denial), that the evaluation would determine, without dispute, that their products were better and our products had to be eliminated.

When the evaluation did not turn out the way they had wanted, then it had been time for euthanasia. How do you euthanize in merged companies? Eliminate the products of the minority party to break their will. First, the new management took control of the **Dumb** product lines: within a few months, it was announced that those products were no longer for sale. Not long after, with the **Dumb** products gone, the need for **Dumb** expertise was too, and teams of **Dumb** people were rounded up and either eliminated or placed in positions of irrelevance.

Guidelines for Success

You can't change the fact that you're in the minority political party and your products are going to play second fiddle. They were not created by the people in charge. You are outmatched. The fight is not fair when you are in the minority party, because you are not in charge. Flanking is the only strategy. How do you flank?

1. **Don't Be Better, Be Different**—Your products will never be better than the party in power's, so don't argue that they are. Position your product(s) as filling a need that can't possibly be solved by the majority party's products. Dig deep to find the differences if necessary. However, this may only prolong your product's death as they try to figure out how to duplicate these differences.

2. **Be Honest**—Don't waste your time making claims for your product that are not true. It only makes you look like a troublemaker and will give you the shortcut out the door, or at least to becoming ostracized. Besides, they're going to kill your products anyway. Keep your dignity: tell the truth.

3. **Focus on Winning**—You could spend an eternity lamenting your product's death. Don't. All the significant products in any category, in any market, are roughly equivalent. Don't get too attached to the products of your creation, because it only causes pain. Focus on the business and the fact that the more products—of either party's—you sell, the more money you make. Remember, they're just products, not your children.

6

The Truth of Attrition: Rightsizing Is the First Big Victory in All Mergers

When your merger is first announced, both management teams will typically make an initial announcement that there are no plans for layoffs or RIF's (reductions in force). Unfortunately, this is a lie. Attempting to keep everyone in the merger would make sense because surely the reason to merge was "to combine the best of both companies and leverage the synergies of complementing technologies, and people, to create something better in whole than the two individual companies." But you already read "The Truth of Addition", and you should know by now that this is a Utopian view. Phrases like "there are no plans" are used because they allow plausible deniability—"We had no *plans* to do this originally, but unfortunately, due to the business environment, we had to change our plans." Believe me, reduction in force is always in the plan, and somebody will be packing their bags before it is over, you can count on it.

First and foremost, remember this is business, and although you probably won't see too many intelligent business decisions during the course of the merger transition, some jobs will be lost simply to clean the house of Democrats and Republicans deemed a liability to the party. The "powers that be" know that the turmoil of the merger will cause a major disruption in the money-making machine, and that they will ultimately still be accountable to shareholders—or, in our case, new owners who are looking for a return on their investment. The merged company will have overlap which cannot be sustained while maintaining profitability.

Since growth will be negligible and most likely negative for the first year, reducing cost is a fantastic way to make your numbers look better. In the media-savvy world we live in, this is known as "rightsizing." You have to hand it to the spin doctor who made old-fashioned layoffs sound like such a positive thing.

Rightsizing to reduce cost may come in many ways, but the first usually targets the largest expense on the books—payroll. Yes, they may say that everybody is going to keep their jobs, but any right-minded individual should be able to see through this smoke-screen and recognize that with all of the overlap and duplication, jobs will have to be reconciled. Rightsizing usually happens in the fall so that management has time to figure out who has to go, and so they can write it off at the end of the year.

Fortunately, if you are deemed a threat to power, you have a chance to survive during the rightsizing selection process. Keeping really talented Democrats on the payroll prohibits them from going to competitors. For this reason, they favor ostracism—ignoring troublemakers who they are not ready to get rid of just yet. Ostracism stops disliked employees from going to competitors, but still eliminates their power. This serves to calm fears among the ranks of power and reduces any threat these employees may pose. Employees in the greatest danger of losing their jobs are those below the management level, typically in positions that are deemed unnecessary, or those whose expertise is of no threat to the Republicans and no benefit to their competitors.

For the **Dumb** employees, the reconciliation started with the sales force, probably because the basic nature of sales people is organized around meeting or exceeding a sales quota any way possible. Soon after the merger there was a mad scramble within the Republican sales force for control of revenue-generating Democratic accounts. The Republicans, after all, had quotas to make. Once these accounts had been taken from the Democrats and replaced with low revenue-generating accounts formerly managed by Republicans, Democrat sales people had a hard time making their quotas, and it was easy to place them on the RIF list.

This strategy, combined with the fact that the **Dumb** products had been planned for elimination, further substantiated the claim that **Dumb** people—who presumably knew how to sell only **Dumb** products—were no longer needed. Within two years of the merger, most of the **Dumb** sales force and sales management had been pushed out the door. Subsequently, this action recursively helped to eliminate the **Dumb** products. With no one to sell them, the decline of new license revenue for these products led to their cancellation.

In addition to a reduction of the sales force came a reduction of those actually producing and supporting the products. Given that the **Dumb** products were going to die, and the **Dumb** sales people had been eliminated for the most part, there was no need for **Dumb** development staff. Most of the **Dumb** development and support staff were given their walking papers at the same time.

Of course, the new company will evaluate all options to wrench out costs like eliminating duplication of assets as I mentioned earlier. For example, Dumber did not need duplicate facilities from both companies in each city. So of course, buildings will be consolidated.

When it came to travel expenses and budget, I and many other Democrats quickly found out that I had to get approval from practically everyone in upper management including the CEO, while for the most part, the party in power could travel anywhere for any reason. The downside was that the approval process that had been put in place to keep costs down had actually made things worse. People, who did travel, had paid more to do so because waiting for management approval forced most plane tickets to be purchased on short notice at higher ticket prices. Others had received travel approvals after appointment dates had passed.

As for the rest of the employees in the Democrat world, their fate was also up in the air, and for obvious reasons. There was certainly no need for two IT departments, HR departments, finance departments, legal departments, or product development teams. You get the picture.

The big day for reduction in force will be coming. If you're lucky, the new management will do it all at once so at least you will know if you had survived, making it easier to feel that your job is secure. **Dumber,** however, had been merciless.

They had had so many mass layoffs that you could not even keep track of who had been let go. This tactic is far worse, because it is another will-breaker for those who survive. It is no fun to watch or hear about your friends being shown the door. Those who still have jobs are left with the task of accomplishing more with less, all the while living in fear that their day is coming.

Guidelines for Success

So what's the lesson? Keep your ear to the ground and a finger to the wind. Read the tea leaves. However you put it, my advice is simple—be prepared! Here are a few tips to help you through the process.

1. **Keep Your Eye on Opportunities**—Look for other organizations in the company where you might be politically aligned, and hedge your bets as to who is going to win in the shuffle of the deck. It's not a bad idea to consider leaving your comfort zone to get in with an organization that has already been sent down the tracks with a commitment to success from the executive management team.

2. **Find a Political Majority Sponsor**—Political alignment with a majority sponsor never hurts. Alignment with someone who deems you valuable can save your career, but can ultimately limit where you can go. If there is no clear way out and you have a good relationship with your current political minority management, stay in their organization. But know that the entire organization is at risk of elimination.

3. **Find Another Job**—I know this is a bit obvious. But many times when you leave a company, if you're gone long enough, you can come back to a higher position. This can backfire, however, if management doesn't change in the period you are gone. In that case, you may be viewed not only as a political minority, but as desperate traitor.

4. **Lie Low**—Find a position that is out of the mainstream of controversy. This is typically a job that is viewed by the party in power as unimportant. I managed to do this for years by working with a product that was not a large revenue generator. I was able to do my job and make an impact, all while many Republicans thought I'd been let go. Fortunately for me, I hid out long enough for new management to come in from the outside, see my talent, and move me to a position of real value. The downside to this strategy is that irrelevant roles can easily be eliminated, so be careful.

7

The Truth of Loyalty: Old Boys Never Die, They Just Network

Once an executive team is put into place, the rest of the organization flows naturally into place, like a pure mountain stream slowly making its way to the sea. Seriously, though, each branch of the organizational chart inherits the attributes of the political party at its origin. It doesn't take a rocket scientist to figure out that if a Republican holds the position at the top, then the majority of the organization, and especially the key positions, will be filled by Republicans. This is similar to how the President of the United States replaces high-ranking members of the other party with members of his own soon after the election.

There are exceptions, however, and occasionally you will find a member of the opposing party in a management role. Self-preservation usually compels managers in this situation to fill subordinate positions with other members of their own party. They have to stick together because there is safety in numbers. The sad part is that no matter how good or talented these people are, they will be considered troublemakers whose political power must be kept in check.

If you remember, I mentioned that only three of the eleven key roles in the organization were given to **Dumb** people. The Democrat COO from **Dumb** had been made head of marketing. Our old Democrat head of marketing from **Dumb** had been placed directly below him and was responsible for strategic marketing. These two guys had actually played key roles in the acquisition and merger of our two companies by **Big Brother**, and I'm sure they had gone into this merger with hope for the future. They had respectfully been given a marketing organization of Republicans and Democrats and had been charged with putting a new marketing strategy in place.

Let's start with the head of marketing. He had sort of a brash personality and was a classic straight shooter—a real "get things done" kind of guy. His aggressive style had not been very popular even within the **Dumb** ranks. However, he had been very good at instigating change, and he had done a tremendous job of energizing **Dumb** and polishing it up to be sold. Nevertheless, if **Dumb** people hadn't liked him much, you can imagine what the **Dumber** Republicans thought of an unruly Democrat like this guy.

Our head of marketing had numerous Republicans in his ranks, one of whom was close friends with the President. This high ranking Republican also happened to be the old head of marketing for **Dumber**. Needless to say, he had a chip on his shoulder because he hadn't been chosen as the new head of marketing. It was obvious within fifteen minutes that this Republican would never tolerate working for a Democrat, and within six months, he managed to use his political clout to force the top Democrat and head of marketing out of the company.

After the head of marketing had been forced out, the next-highest ranking **Dumb** guy heading up strategic marketing was asked to replace him. This guy was one of the most likable guys you could ever meet. In fact, even the Republicans liked him. Unfortunately, he didn't have this book to reference, or he would have known that his days were numbered. No matter how likable he was, there was no way a Republican would be subservient to a Democrat. Six months passed before they stripped him of his power and budget, and finally gave his job to a Republican. He had been ostracized and his organization rid of Republicans, such that his team of Democrats could be isolated and politically controlled. This left the team powerless to influence anything in the business, and with no real marketing budget, they were reduced to making PowerPoint slides.

As for me and my role, the transfer of power occurred rather quickly. My job was quickly divided amongst the Republicans and I was left with the smallest piece. So instead of doing work that helped to generate three hundred million dollars a year in revenue, I was now responsible for doing work that supported twenty-seven million dollars in revenue. Naturally it was a blow to my ego, and it took a number of months to get over, but I ultimately did—and then I put together some of my best work to date. What was the reward for my efforts? I was moved to an even smaller new role. The process was repeated more than once; after drastically increasing revenue from a project previously deemed insignificant, I would be moved to a still smaller role and the newly profitable project I left given to a Republican. I was, finally relegated to a position supporting the generation of just over one million dollars in revenue per year.

I wasn't alone: the Republican majority was slowly appointing fellow Republicans to fill the jobs of Democrats throughout the company. In one case, a **Dumb** sales rep had even been told by his new **Dumber** manager that he "was not from the right lineage," and his accounts were realigned to a

Dumber sales guy. I love the term "realigned." I believe the correct translation is something like, "We don't like you very much, so we're taking everything you've worked hard for over the past several years, and giving it to someone we do like."

Of course, the new management didn't always feel the need for indirection. Sometimes they were frankly hostile. I often found myself subject to the rude outpourings of Republicans, who felt that they had the right to accost Democrats whenever they wanted to. Why wouldn't they? They were in charge—in their minds indefinitely. This is where power becomes danger-ous. When people with power feel beyond reprise, they do bad things. Look at Nero, or Caligula.

Of course, the Republicans didn't have quite as much power as the Roman emperors had, and their excesses were correspondingly less spectacular. Sometimes, however, their behavior was still quite disturbing. Early on in the merger, I had traveled to Detroit for a meeting to help Democrats learn more about the Republican products. The fact that we hadn't been having any meetings to help Republicans learn about Democrat products should have been a sign of things to come. The meeting had lasted two days and had soon disintegrated into a discussion about nothing, so I decided to answer an important e-mail during what I thought was a break in the action. This was apparently a bad idea. One of my new col-leagues, whom I had just met the day before, literally screamed at me for not paying attention to the conversation. Expletives flew through the air like shrapnel: the tongue-lashing was far worse than anything I had ever received from my parents, and was delivered in a forum of some fifteen other professionals. I'm still in shock when I think about it.

I was angry, humiliated, and unsure how to deal with the situation. I needed to tell my manager what had happened, but thought it should be done face to face. The following week, I traveled to another meeting with my manager and—coincidentally—the screamer's manager. Upon entering the meeting, his manager had said, "I heard my boy was out of line last week." I found that pleasantly surprising, and responded with, "Yeah, it was a little out of hand." Just then my manager entered the room, catching the end of my sentence; "Oh, I don't believe it for a second," he said, "I've known him for twenty years, and he'd never do something like that."

Even though everyone had clearly heard what had happened, and there had been more than a dozen witnesses, my manager squashed the whole incident by claiming he didn't believe it. So what could I say? The issue was dead. This is the Truth of Loyalty in action. If your manager is from a different political party, no matter what you do for him, or how much he likes you, he will always defend his party before you.

Similar behavior was exhibited throughout the company leading to Democrats in leadership positions being replaced with Republicans. There were two exceptions. They had had to keep our head of Nerdy research and development. Not because he was good, which he was, but because the Republicans hadn't known anything about Nerdy. Similarly, a Democrat had been left in charge of **Disaster**, because it was considered dead, and somebody had to be left in the lame duck position. This arrangement was designed to ensure that **Disaster** customers would continue to give us ongoing revenue for keeping the product running until we could convert them to the Republican product. Since few **Disaster** customers were converting to the Republican product **NewComplex**, it appeared that this job would exist for quite some time.

What's the lesson here? The minority party cannot be responsible for successful products. All things successful must be owned by the Republican majority for fear that Democrats might actually gain power. All Democrats, in a Republican majority, will at some point be relieved of their successful projects, which will neatly be handed to a Republican who needs to own something. The real beauty of it, if you remember what I said about who writes history (the winners), is that over time, the new Republican owners will be credited for your successes.

The Republicans' record of successes will mysteriously reach backward in time, and your new colleagues will take credit for inheriting clients they actually inherited with the merger. The Republicans in my company were certainly pleased with themselves for "winning" **Dumb**'s marquee customers.

So don't kid yourself, and wipe away those aspirations of sliding into a role of power. Even if you manage to grab a key management role in the organization, it most likely will only be a matter of time until you are ostracized for being a Democrat and replaced by a Republican. Soon after, they will lay claim to your successes.

Guidelines for Success

Persecution is always a tough thing to overcome. In many cases, the best thing you can do is keep your head down and your mouth shut. I was not very good at this in the beginning, but over time I found that fighting the political battle only led to more stress in my life and countless hours of wasted energy.

1. **Take a Small Role**—I allowed myself to take a smaller role (not for less money or lower title, although this may be necessary), but still working for a Democrat. This enabled me to get off the beaten path, into a role that the Republicans really didn't care too much about, and reporting to a leader who treated me with respect. Because I stayed under the radar, I found that the Republicans left me alone. When I ran into them, they frequently expressed surprise that I still worked at the company. Four years later I was still there, and was actually making a little more money, although this path had not been without sacrifice to my short-term goals and career. It is important to remember your career is a long race and occasionally, you might get forced to take a time out along the way by taking a less significant role. But don't worry. Things will

change in your organization every six months or so. The challenge is to know when to start pursuing your goals again.

2. **Be Open to Change**—Don't be afraid of change. You might actually find that you like your new role. You might learn new things which will broaden your resume.

8

The Truth of Trust: The Root of Trust Is Us—and You Are Them

The most painful aspect of the power structure in the new regime is that somehow, all of the members of the reigning party, regardless of their position in the organization, will feel and act as if they have the right of approval, or veto power, over everything you do. This is because it is very difficult for the Republican majority to trust the Democrats.

When I was handed my new assignment, I was amazed to discover that I had to work with a cross-functional team made up entirely of Republicans. I was open-minded and looking forward to doing some good work, but had quickly learned that no one on this cross-functional team had any interest in helping a Democrat be successful. In the Republican mind, Democrats were merely children who must be kept on a leash to prevent them from doing too much damage. Democrats could not be trusted. The team operated like a one-man action team with six person reviewers.

Here was how it went. I did the work, and then spent endless hours reviewing with the team, who chose not to review my work independently beforehand so as to not waste their time. In these review meetings, I would go over my work in detail, while they shot holes in it. These review processes would continue for months at a time, and in most cases, would continue until the task or ultimate deliverable we had been reviewing no longer had value, or would simply get vetoed by the Republicans. The vetoes would often come from people who had no interaction with my team or our projects, but had heard secondhand that a Democrat was trying to do something that didn't support the Republican party line. My work, no matter how good, could not be accepted because I wasn't trusted by the Republicans.

I once had a vice president in another organization (Republican of course) veto my work and cancel the project. Did that mean that I had power over their organization's work? Of course not. I never figured out why one organization had the right to review, critique, and veto another organization's work. The HR department wasn't holding software code reviews, and marketing didn't review the work of the finance department.

I played football when I was younger which gave me some ideas about teamwork that just don't work in a merged company. I never really spent much time making sure that the quarterback knew how to take the snap or that the safety knew how to cover the correct zone. We were a team. I trusted that every man knew how to do his job. It was this sense of trust that enabled the team to function.

Of course, this should translate to business as well; a well-oiled business machine is built on trust. Marketing must trust that product development is writing the software properly, and likewise, product development must trust that marketing is creating effective programs to sell it. Workers assume that sales knows how to sell, HR knows how to put together benefits programs, and the mail room knows how to deliver their mail. But the Republicans I knew must never have played football.

In this new organization, the word "team" was used, shall we say, rather loosely. Unfortunately, since there was no trust, there was no team, and since there was no team, the Republicans forced us to the bottom of the food chain. The corporate culture was very similar to any number of the two-tiered societies that have existed throughout history. Welcome to feudalism—you've just become a serf.

My only source of sanity was that I wasn't the only Democrat who had to work on a cross-functional team like this. One of my co-workers in a similar situation to me coined one of my favorite business terms ever—The Revenue Prevention Team, or RPT. The RPT was composed of Republicans dedicated to making sure Democrats accomplished nothing. That's right, the cross-functional teams seemed to be organized around the idea that because Democrats could not be trusted, they had to be stopped—even if that meant the prevention of good work that brought in revenue for the company.

Some days I felt like I was working in a spy movie. In a conspiracy more far-reaching than I could even fathom, teams of Republicans were secretly gathered in a subversive plot to prevent revenue for the sake of stopping the Democrats from achieving any form of success. This was the best explanation I could devise for the secrecy surrounding the financial goals of both the business and its organizations. The RPT was naturally top secret, and no Republicans must ever be held accountable. The only events that could be recorded were those that highlighted Democratic failure.

Lack of trust by the Republicans also led to them controlling the autonomy of Democrats whenever possible. This lack of autonomy became clear to me when our new VP asked me to take on a new role. I was given this opportunity only because this person was a new VP, brought in from the outside, which meant he had not been either a Democrat or a Republican. For the sake of keeping the affiliations straight, let's say he belonged to the Green Party. Being Green, he didn't give a damn about the political battle between the Democrats and the Republicans. Because he had no political alignment with the Republicans, he decided to give me a shot at leading a team with real value.

At first, the role of managing this team had sounded all right, but it didn't really afford me any growth. I had actually been in a similar group back in the **Dumb** days a decade before, so I understood the role well, but I wasn't very excited about going back and managing people. I would have to trade much of the creative work I did for issue management.

But then I realized that the work this group was supposed to perform had never been done at **Dumber**—or at least not well. In other words, this work had been desperately needed. This was a great opportunity for me. I knew how to do this job with my eyes closed. I had a good team of people who had done great work in the past, but due to lack of leadership, had been doing all of the wrong things where this assignment was concerned. The expectation level had been set very low based on the limited success for this role in the past, and my management team had given me some basic deliverables for the next year, which had been very conservative.

So the stage was set: this was the no-lose situation I'd been looking for all of my life. It was incredible. I could lay down a basic plan, apply some basic leadership skills, set expectations low, and then over-deliver.

It was sort of like Marvin Lewis taking over coaching the Cincinnati Bengals in 2003. At the time, the Bengals had been God-Awful (as my old football coach used to say). They had just racked up thirteen consecutive seasons without a winning record and had actually been voted the worst sports franchise, of any sport, in the history of the world. For the record, that was unfair. Consider teams like the Detroit Lions, the Phoenix Cardinals, and the Cleveland Browns, who have yet to go to a Super Bowl. The Bengals have gone to two, and they barely lost both.

Many people wondered why Marvin Lewis would want to take over such a bad team with such bad management. In reality, it was the best opportunity that could have ever been laid before Marvin Lewis. It was a no-lose situation. Had he come to the Bengals and continued the losing streak, it would have been blamed on the franchise, the management, and the players.

The fact is that there had been nowhere for Marvin Lewis and the Bengals to go but up. Winning six or seven games his first season would still have left the Bengals with a losing record, but it would have been a major turn around from the usual two or three wins. But Marvin and the Bengals went on to have 8-8 seasons in both of his first two years with the team, and the turn around had begun. Marvin Lewis was becoming respected; since his 11-6 third season, he's being talked about as a genius.

In contrast, if Marvin had taken a job with a winning team, it would have been much harder for him to make noticeable improvements. When you're on top, the only place to go is down.

I had taken the job on the same premise. There had been nowhere to go but up. I would make my team look like studs, and we would all be rewarded with huge bonuses and piles of stock options.

And that was exactly what happened—except for the bonus and the stock options. But we'll get back to that in a minute. We rolled out our first set of deliverables in two months, to enormous praise, and our second set six months later to similar accolades. Our company had never seen anything like it. They were completely blown away. It was outstanding.

But even making that kind of impact could not get me into the inner sphincter—the Circle of Trust. When it came time for me to bring a new person onto the team, I did not have the authority to determine what we should pay him, let alone the power to negotiate the deal.

When it came to dollars and cents, I had no say. Instead, I had to act as a middleman messenger between the new employee and my boss. Playing the middleman in salary negotiations isn't fun, and in this case we ended up making an offer that had to be retracted because it was disapproved by the president of the company (who also had to approve the purchase of jumbo paper clips). The final offer was far worse than what this person had originally accepted, so the guy was disgruntled from the very beginning, because his salary had been taken away from him before he even started. It wasn't pretty.

In the entire time I was with the merged company, I was never involved in the management of budgets, raises, or anything to do with money. In fact, during yearly reviews, I was asked which of my guys would be most deserving of a bonus if there was some extra money to hand out. First of all it had been offensive that my team, who had over-delivered as I had mentioned earlier, had been an afterthought when it came to compensation. At any rate, the person I had recommended didn't even get the bonus. My boss took it upon himself to rank my team himself, and gave the bonus to the guy I had ranked as #2 in my group. So why had he asked me at all? Since I had no say in compensation, I certainly didn't feel like

I needed to handle the performance reviews—my boss should have done those too. But you know that didn't happen, because that took real work.

As for my own bonus, it was a joke and an insult coming in at 1.7 percent of my salary. It was the worst bonus I had ever received, excluding the prior four years, when I got no bonus at all. Unfortunately, compensation too is tied to trust. As soon as these two companies had merged, my raises and bonuses had pretty much stopped. That was tough for a guy who had been used to a 20 percent bonus, and 3000–6000 stock options a year. But when you're Democrat in a Republican organization, you don't get perks. That's the bottom line.

I had a performance review a couple years into the merger, and I was given an average rating—because, I was told, my boss didn't really know what I had done that year. I went in with data proving that I had actually helped increase revenue 211 percent, but it had had no impact on my review. I went on to say that I deserved a bonus and a raise based on the metrics of my success, or at least because I had not received either since we had merged. My boss had told me I was not eligible for a bonus since I had not scored above average on the review. So essentially, I had gotten no bonus because my boss hadn't known what I had worked on that year. But this is life when you're a Democrat in a Republican-controlled Congress.

Guidelines for Success

I found the Republican's lack of trust in me one of the hardest things to deal with. I am an honest person, and have always prided myself on doing the right thing. Ultimately, you have to be happy with yourself.

1. **Work Within Your Means**—You can't change that you are not trusted, so do what you can with what you've got. You may not be given a budget, but you can still accomplish things, although they may feel small and unfulfilling.

2. **Swallow Your Pride**—Don't let pride get in the way of doing your job. You can't change what the Republican majority thinks of you. Remember that sticks and stones may break your bones, but names can never hurt you. Ignore how they treat you—if you want to keep your job.

3. **Define Your Own Standards**—Don't let the Republican opinion be how you measure yourself. You be the judge. You have your own personal standards. You know when you are doing well or poorly, so hold yourself accountable, and rejoice within about your successes.

9

The Truth of Fear: The Primal Instinct of Fear Will Decide Who Gets Ostracized

What happens in merged businesses is not much different than what happened on *Wild Kingdom*. Surely we all recall watching as Marlin Perkins rode in the helicopter while the fearless Jim (what was his last name anyway?) remained on the ground to study the primitive social structures of the lions or baboons. If you were paying attention, the baboons' social structure ultimately came down to a couple of type A males who had to establish who was going to rule the roost. These baboons were concerned almost entirely with each other, primarily out of the most basic instinct: fear. Dominant baboons really only fear other dominant baboons, and the basic fear of being relegated to a lower status drives them to confront one another, even though the confrontation could bring about their own deaths.

Surely, in an advanced society such as our own, given our belief that all people are created equal and that working together is preferable to alienation and conflict, intelligent human beings would never engage in such primitive tactics to avoid losing stature—right? Actually, the winning party in a merger or acquisition can out-baboon the baboons.

Remember that a merged company has lots of overlap and lots of unnecessary jobs that will ultimately get reconciled. Maybe the Republicans were smarter than the Democrats, or at least smarter than I was, because they figured out almost immediately which Democrats had the most political influence, and they acted quickly to neutralize their power.

In the merged society, it is not good to appear to hold influence if you are a Democrat. You might be an up-and-comer with unprecedented talent in the Democratic party and a resume that reads like an induction speech for a lifetime achievement award at the Grammy's, Oscars, and Football Hall of Fame combined. But that resume will serve best tucked in your pocket, in case you need it for your next job. It can only serve to make you the object of fear for some Republican whose actions are driven by self-preservation.

It had never occurred to me that these forces were at work, so I was blindsided when the Republicans came after me. I've mentioned that, at least in my mind, I had been an up-and-comer, and at the onset of this merger I thought life would be great—and naturally I would continue in the direction my career was currently taking me. I was wrong. I often speculate on what specific action put a target on my back. In actuality, it had probably been several things I had done in our first major assembly for the newly merged company. It had been a public forum of well over one hundred of the merged company's top Republicans and Democrats.

I had presented at that first meeting of the minds. I had started with an ice breaker—"I have to say, I feel a lot of love in this room." That was a little joke I'd learned from Chevy Chase, and it was well received. Little did I know what a big joke it actually was. I had gone on to give one of my better presentations; the **Big Brother** people in the room had come up to comment that it had been the only presentation they had understood all day. There had even been one Republican from **Dumber** who had come up to congratulate me on a great presentation. I'm sure he had been drawn and quartered later that night by the Republicans for breaking ranks. But although I thought I had hit a home run, I had really just put a target on my back.

It hadn't helped that I had been seen associating closely that day with the rest of **Dumb**'s executive management, most of which had been targeted for elimination from day one. I was guilty by association, a kid taken under their wing.

The presentation itself had probably gone too well. Good oration is a powerful tool, which can prove very scary to those in power. Showing that you can persuade and influence people is a sure way to get yourself killed. So be careful—you too could be one good presentation in a large forum away from being targeted.

My perceived youth had certainly put me at a disadvantage. I had clearly been the youngest guy in the room at every merger strategy meeting. In a merged company, someone in their late thirties doesn't fit well in a management team of guys who are thirty-year-men in the company. Although I had been in the business for fifteen years, and had enough experience myself to go toe to toe with these guys, my perceived youth had only served to amplify the fears of the Republicans who were now in charge.

After awhile, anything I said was ignored as if it was not credible; eventually, they wouldn't even acknowledge my comments—is this mike on? These ding-dongs would turn and look at me as if I had called their mother a bad name and were wondering who had invited the college student. They then turned back around and continued their conversations as if what I had to say couldn't possibly have had any relevance to anything.

Guidelines for Success

I'm not asking you to change who you are, or to eliminate all of the skills that have made you successful, but unfortunately, you have to make concessions somewhere. Yes this is painful, especially if you are a type A person who takes pride in winning and making a difference. So there is a simple strategy that will dramatically increase your chances of surviving this storm, commonly referred to as "flying below the radar." The more you look like a threat, the worse off you will be. There are several key things that will cause fear in the Republican majority and must be avoided:

1. **Negative comments about the party in power**

2. **Excluding the party in power from discussions**

3. **Successful accomplishment of a task not managed by or inclusive of the party in power. Always include the party in power and let them have the credit**

4. **Publicly voicing opinions that oppose those of the party in power—keep your mouth shut**

5. **Appearing to be an up-and-comer—old dogs hate new tricks**

6. **Attempting to teach something to the party in power—once again, keep your mouth shut**

7. **Mentioning how the minority party used to do things—how you used to do things will not matter**

8. **Volunteering to lead activities—sit back and remember that you are on the bench**

9. **Having review meetings without including the party in power**

10. **Wearing or displaying items with old company logos. Leave them at home—those days are gone**

If you choose to disregard any of the above, you are taking your life in your own hands. Tread lightly.

10

The Truth of Denial:
The Right Way Is Our Way

By now, these Truths are probably giving you a feeling of déjà vu: is anyone reminded of older siblings, bullies, or the various cliques at school? Sadly enough, these Truths are nothing more than the essence of human nature in action. We are only mortals, living on instincts that we fight so hard against to create a better society.

Sorry—I got a little philosophical for a second.

But the fact is that the party in power in a merger or acquisition has a common faith in what they do. It is only natural for them to want to continue doing things the way that is familiar and most comfortable to them. In business, this means there is no chance that they will ever even consider what the minority party thinks, believes, or does when it comes to making decisions. All operations of the newly formed business will be driven and run the Republican way—no ifs, ands, or buts about it. The Republicans do things the right way. "If the Democrats did things the right way, then they would be in charge."

I actually had some jerk say that to me. The discussion occurred early in the merger—and no, it wasn't that "we should have been kicking your ass for years" product development guy. But believe me, this guy had been thinking that too. This was one of his golf-and-drinks cronies, a guy in one of those deputy positions where you're never required to deliver anything or make goals, but just do what the big guy tells you.

The same guy went on to say—with complete confidence and conviction, with piercing eyes as if to lance my soul—"You knew **Disaster** had to go. **Complex** is just superior technology, and if it weren't, you'd have bought us."

Last time I checked, these losers hadn't bought us—**Big Brother** had. But **Dumber** had been put in charge, and so they might as well have bought us.

The philosophy that the Republicans do things the right way will permeate every level of the organization, from product development, to marketing, to HR, to IT. If I had a dime for every time I heard "that's not how we do things here," or "we've never done that before," or "we always do it this way," I'd be sitting on a beach somewhere sipping a cocktail full-time. But part of faith is blind—believing you're right even when there are no facts that support your belief.

The Republicans in our company truly believed that their products had been the best, to the point that they would not listen to or accept any constructive criticism. This was where things started to get dangerous, because this denial of reality had extended far beyond not listening to your own people and now included ignoring your competitors.

Both of our Tech products had been old and outdated. Over the past ten years, a newer, easier-to-use, and less-expensive wave of products had come into the market, and had slowly been eating the established product's lunch, including ours.

These new products had made significant gains in market share over ten years and had become the products of choice in the market. But rather than acknowledge where the market had gone, the Republicans found it much easier to continue to live in denial and to tell themselves that they had a better product. Unfortunately, in business it doesn't matter what you tell yourself about your products. What matters is what people want to buy.

As I mentioned before, the Republican product **Complex** was a VCR that they were very proud of, and they would go to all lengths to ignore the fact that the market had shifted to new technology—DVD players. We actually had a DVD player—it had been our Tech system called **Blacksheep**, which had been a product **Dumber** acquired from one of our competitors, **Loserbird,** years back. But since it hadn't been created by the Republicans, it could never be a flagship product. So all recommendations to make **Blacksheep** core to our market strategy had been ignored.

When it came to our Regulator product, it was the same. As I mentioned earlier, the Democrat's Regulator product, **Antiquated**, had been the leader in the market, with more than ten times the number of customers than the Republican product **Halfbaked**. But the Republicans had been in denial. They hadn't believed those numbers, and whenever we had discussions about the numbers, they would try to skew the numbers, or make up new ones to make the Republican product look like it had had just as many customers and had generated as much revenue. Additionally, the Republicans would claim that customers had not been using **Antiquated** or that the numbers suggested by the Democrats and the market analysts had been wrong.

They had to deny these numbers, or else they wouldn't be able to justify why they had been killing the Democrat products and the Democrat organization.

But denial goes far beyond just evaluating products. It also came into play when evaluating people. The poor performance of a Republican in the organization, or the outstanding performance of a Democrat, always had to be overlooked.

One of our vice presidents of sales, for example, was an outstanding leader and businessman. His team consistently made his numbers quarter after quarter, while most other sales regions had been setting new records for consecutive quarters of not making quota. This guy also happened to be a Democrat. So what's a Republican to do? What else but claim that the only reason they had not been making their numbers was that the Democrat team had been taking their deals and revenue, which would account for their better performance.

No investigation is necessary when you're the party in power. What you believe must be true—and if it's not, you don't want to know. The party in power will deny anything that isn't the way they want it to be. This is the essence of denial.

The downside of denial is that you can easily set yourself up for massive harm: "No, I don't have a drinking problem." Substitute a drug problem, a smoking problem, an anger-management problem, or a spending problem if you like. Pick your poison—all of them lead to ruin of one form or another.

Businesses are not immune to the effects of denial. Denial in the case of the American Auto Industry was the misguided belief that Americans would continue to buy American, no matter what. To help fill the void when American car sales declined over the past few decades, GM bought AVIS and National, and Ford once owned Hertz to increase their car sales. On the other hand, GM and Ford were very successful truck companies and were well established as the leaders in the truck market. In fact they sold so many trucks that they also had to utilize the car rental companies to have a place to dump the additional cars they were forced to produce to raise their average fuel economy per vehicle to meet the government's Corporate Average Fuel Economy (CAFE) requirements.

So when fuel prices soared in 2005, I think most of the American Auto Industry was caught in denial that they had a problem. But when Americans stopped buying American trucks in favor of better fuel economy, the bottom fell out of the industry. With both truck and care sales down, I guarantee that the American auto worker is no longer in denial, but the road to recovery will be long and costly in the form of lost jobs.

Dumber's day is coming. Blind faith in anything is dangerous. It reminds me of one of my favorite quotes from *Jaws*, where Matt Hooper (played by Richard Dreyfuss) says something to the Mayor of Amity like, "It is clear to me that you are going to continue to ignore this problem until it swims up and bites you in the ass." Whether it is your products, your people, or even your processes, denial of your problems will eventually come back and, like Jaws, bite you in the end.

Guidelines for Success

Outside of intervening, there is very little you can do when someone is in denial. And in a newly acquired or merged company, intervention is not a good idea. The party in power doesn't really care what you think if you are in the minority party. They won't believe that your opinion is independent or unbiased. They think you are out to take their job. Advice from the minority party is the last thing they want. The party in power will have to overcome, or stumble across, reality on their own. You only have to hope they do it before they put the company in so much jeopardy that jobs such as your own get eliminated. Here are some basic guidelines I'd recommend for survival in the society of denial:

1. **If You Can't Say Anything Nice, Don't Say Anything at All**—Thumper's mother was right. Whether in your personal life or in a political battle during a merger, negative comments only make matters worse. The mere suggestion that a Republican is mistaken or in denial is a great way to get escorted from the building on the next RIF. Besides, you might make them cry.

2. **Don't Brag about Your Products**—they won't believe you anyway. Besides, it's actually kind of fun, human

nature being what it is, to watch people in denial chase their tails trying to figure out what's wrong.

3. **Use Competitor Capabilities to Get Your Point Across**—It is far worse to say that the minority party product does something better than a majority party product than it is to say that a competitor does something better than the majority party product. This is a call to action for the majority party who can handle responding to competition, just not the minority party.

4. **Yet Again, Keep Your Mouth Shut**—Remember, there are no awards to people who bring up problems, especially Democrats.

11

The Final Analysis

I'm sure by now you've probably concluded I'm just an angry young man struggling to deal with what has happened to my career. Some of that may be a true, but you must give these lessons some respect, and be sensible enough to heed my warnings. The truth of my situation lends credibility to these stories. I am not a guy who is talking from the bowels of the organization or who was let go. Keep in mind that I held an upper-level position, and I was extremely well paid. So there is some credibility to my claims. I am not seeking revenge or reprisal, but rather am looking to share what has been one of the biggest learning experiences of my life.

I'm sure you know someone who has been through M&A, so I encourage you to investigate and confirm how well these Truths ring with others who have been through this same situation. No matter what, there are no easy answers for the road that lies ahead. I can only hope that you have learned some lessons to help guide you through the process and salvage your career and avoid my mistakes. "If we ignore our past, we are doomed to repeat it." So hang tough, and best of luck.

978-0-595-40208-3
0-595-40208-9

Printed in the United States
71184LV00001B/105